EVERYTHING'S FOR SALE

How To Grow Rich By Giving Away Everything For Free

Wisdom Kwati

Ordering Details

To place orders or for details of discounts for bulk purchases by organizations or groups either for support, gift, training packages, fundraising, or any other educational purposes, contact the author via email: wisdomkwati@gmail.com. Follow Wisdom Kwati on all social media platforms and visit his website: www.wisdomkwati.com.

Table of Contents

INTRODUCTION

It is no news that most businesses have long focused on sales and profits as the ultimate measures of success. However, there is a new paradigm that is emerging—one that challenges the status quo and offers a groundbreaking approach to wealth-building. We are currently in a time when everything is for sale, but not in the way you might expect.

In this book, I decided to share conventional wisdom that will get your eyes opened to the extraordinary possibilities that lie in the power of generosity. Gone are the days when success was solely measured by the number of transactions made and revenue generated. The old way of doing business, where profit margins reigned supreme and customers were seen as mere sources of income, has reached its expiration date.

Today, a new era of business is dawning—one that places value creation, customer-centricity, and the spirit of giving at its core. As you read this book, you will discover a fresh perspective that defies common notions of business success. You will learn about the concept of giving away everything for free as a wealth-building strategy—a notion that may seem counterintuitive at first, but one that holds the potential to revolutionize your business and transform your life.

The old way of doing business is fading away, making room for a new era—a future where generosity reigns, and success is measured not just by the size of your bank account, but by the positive impact you create. It's time to embrace this new reality that will change the way you view business, wealth, and the world itself.

Enjoy your read!

Chapter 1
From Selling to Giving

In the past, the traditional way of doing business revolved around the concept of selling. Entrepreneurs and business owners focused on maximizing profits by selling their products or services at the highest possible prices. The primary goal was to make a sale and generate revenue. However, this approach often created a transactional relationship with customers, where the emphasis was on extracting value rather than providing it.

But times have changed, and a paradigm shift is taking place in the business world. This shift is driven by the realization that giving away everything for free can be a powerful strategy for wealth-building and business growth. The concept of giving has gained momentum as entrepreneurs recognize the immense value it brings to their businesses and the profound impact it has on their customers.

By embracing this new approach, you are breaking away from the traditional sales-focused mindset and adopting a mindset of abundance and generosity. Instead of focusing solely on making immediate sales, you are shifting your attention towards building trust, establishing long-term relationships, and creating genuine value for your customers.

Giving away everything for free may seem counterproductive at first glance. After all, how can you make money if you're not charging for your products or services? The key lies in understanding the deeper dynamics at play. When you provide valuable information, resources, and experiences without any immediate monetary exchange, you are building a foundation of goodwill and trust with your audience.

When you freely share your expertise, knowledge, and insights, you position yourself as an authority in your industry. You become a go-to resource for valuable information, and customers begin to perceive you as a trusted advisor rather than just another salesperson. This builds a strong sense of loyalty and credibility, which sets you apart from your competitors.

Giving away everything for free also creates reciprocity. When you offer something of value without expecting anything in return, customers feel a sense of indebtedness. They are more likely to reciprocate by engaging with your business, recommending you to others, and eventually becoming paying customers. This reciprocity fosters a virtuous cycle of trust, loyalty, and exponential growth.

Moreover, the act of giving freely creates a positive and

memorable experience for your customers. It establishes an emotional connection and makes them feel valued and appreciated. This emotional connection translates into long-term customer relationships and customer advocacy, which in turn leads to organic growth through word-of-mouth marketing.

I know that at this point, you are wondering how this would work. I need you to however recognize that giving away everything for free doesn't mean neglecting your own financial well-being. It's about finding the right balance between generosity and monetization. While you may provide valuable information and resources for free, you can still create revenue streams through complementary products or services, premium offerings, collaborations, or even strategic partnerships.

You need to understand that the paradigm shift from selling to giving is a transformative journey. It requires a shift in mindset, a willingness to let go of old beliefs, and a commitment to creating value for your customers. When you embrace this new approach, you are not only creating a thriving business but also contributing to a larger movement of generosity, authenticity, and customer-centricity in the business world.

Embrace the power of giving, and watch as your business flourishes in ways you never thought possible. The opportunities are boundless, and the rewards are immeasurable. It's time to make the paradigm shift and embark on a journey that will change the way you do business forever.

Understanding The Concept Of "Free"

The concept of giving away everything for free as a wealth-building strategy may seem counterintuitive at first, but it is rooted in the power of generosity, reciprocity, and the creation of long-term value. This approach involves providing valuable resources, information, and experiences to your audience without any immediate monetary exchange.

Instead of focusing solely on making immediate sales, the emphasis is on building trust, establishing strong relationships, and creating genuine value for your customers. To achieve this, you need to have these in mind:

Building Trust and Credibility: When you freely share your expertise, knowledge, and insights, you position yourself as an authority in your industry. This builds trust and credibility with your audience, as they perceive you as a reliable source of valuable information. Customers are more likely to engage with your business and consider you as a trusted advisor.

Creating a Loyal Customer Base: When you provide valuable resources or experiences for free, customers feel a sense of reciprocity and gratitude. This emotional connection fosters loyalty and encourages them to support your business. They are more likely to become repeat customers and even advocates who recommend your offerings to others.

Demonstrating Expertise and Differentiation: By giving away valuable content, you showcase your expertise and unique value proposition. This sets you apart from competitors and positions you as a leader in your field. Customers perceive the quality of your free offerings and associate it with the quality they can expect from your paid products or services.

Generating Word-of-Mouth Marketing: When you provide exceptional value for free, customers are more inclined to share their positive experiences with others. This creates a powerful word-of-mouth marketing effect, increasing your brand's visibility and attracting new customers. Positive recommendations from satisfied customers can significantly impact your business's growth.

Establishing Relationships and Customer Loyalty: Giving away everything for free allows you to establish deeper connections with your customers. It demonstrates that you genuinely care about their success and well-being. This fosters long-term relationships, as customers perceive the value you provide and are more likely to engage with your business over time.

Expanding Your Reach and Audience: Free offerings have the potential to reach a broader audience. When people discover the value you provide for free, they become interested in your business and may explore your paid offerings. Additionally, free resources are often shared on social media or through word-of-mouth, exposing your brand to new potential customers.

Upselling and Cross-Selling Opportunities: While you may be giving away valuable resources for free, you can strategically incorporate upselling and cross-selling opportunities within your offerings. For example, you can offer additional premium services or products that complement the free resources. This allows you to generate revenue while still providing significant value.

Building Brand Reputation and Authority: By consistently delivering valuable content and resources for free, you establish a strong brand reputation and authority in your industry. Customers perceive you as a thought leader and go-to resource, which strengthens your position in the market. This can lead to increased opportunities for partnerships, collaborations, and speaking engagements.

Harnessing the Power of Viral Marketing: Exceptional free offerings have the potential to go viral, especially in the age of social media. When people are impressed by the value you provide, they are more likely to share it with their networks. This amplifies your brand's reach, driving organic growth and exposure to a wider audience.

Adaptability and Flexibility: The strategy of giving away everything for free allows you to adapt and evolve with changing market conditions. You can continuously refine and update your free offerings to meet the evolving needs and preferences of your audience. This flexibility enhances your relevance and keeps you at the forefront of your industry.

In summary, giving away everything for free as a wealth-building strategy involves creating value, building trust, and nurturing strong relationships with your audience. It is based on the principle that by freely sharing your knowledge, expertise, and resources, you can attract a loyal customer base, generate positive word-of-mouth, and ultimately drive business growth.

To **implement this strategy effectively**, consider the following:

Clearly Define Your Value: Identify the unique knowledge, expertise, or resources that you can provide for free. Determine how these offerings align with your target audience's needs and preferences. This clarity will ensure that you are delivering value that resonates with your customers.

Consistent and High-Quality Content: Deliver valuable content consistently to build trust and maintain engagement. This can take the form of blog articles, podcasts, videos, webinars, or any other medium that suits your audience. Ensure that your content is of high quality and reflects your expertise, as this will reinforce your credibility.

Understand Your Target Audience: Gain deep

insights into your target audience's pain points, challenges, and aspirations. Tailor your free offerings to address these specific needs and provide solutions. By understanding your audience, you can deliver content that truly resonates and builds a connection

Create a Conversion Funnel: While you are providing free resources, design a clear path for customers to transition to your paid offerings. This can be done through calls-to-action within your free content, offering premium services or products as an extension of the value you provide for free. Guide your audience towards the next step in their journey with you.

Cultivate Relationships: Engage with your audience through various channels, such as social media, email newsletters, or online communities. Respond to their questions, comments, and feedback. Personalize your interactions as much as possible to create a sense of connection and build strong relationships.

Monitor and Measure Results: Track the impact of your free offerings on your business growth. Monitor metrics such as website traffic, social media engagement, lead generation, and conversion rates. Analyze the data to gain insights into what is working and make adjustments as needed.

Evolve and Innovate: Continuously evaluate and improve your free offerings based on customer feedback and market trends. Stay up to date with industry advancements and adjust your strategy accordingly. Innovation and adaptation will ensure that your free offerings remain valuable and relevant over time.

Collaborate and Network: Seek opportunities to collaborate with other experts, influencers, or complementary businesses. Partnering with others can help expand your reach, leverage their audiences, and enhance the value you provide. Collaborations can lead to joint ventures, cross-promotion, and shared resources.

Remember, the goal is to build long-term relationships and establish your brand as a trusted authority. Embrace the mindset of abundance and generosity, understanding that by giving away everything for free, you are investing in the growth and success of your business. As you consistently deliver value, your audience will recognize and appreciate the impact you have on their lives, and this will ultimately translate into financial success and wealth-building opportunities.

Chapter 2

The Power of Generosity

We are in an era when business is highly competitive; where the pursuit of profit often takes center stage. So, there is a transformative force that has the potential to revolutionize your approach—the power of generosity. When you embrace a mindset of giving and focusing on providing value to your customers without expectation, you can unlock a remarkable path to building trust, fostering loyalty, and ultimately achieving long-term success.

When you adopt a generous mindset, you prioritize the needs and interests of your customers above immediate financial gains. You begin to genuinely care about their success and well-being, and you create a positive perception of your brand and establish a strong foundation of trust. To achieve this, pay attention to these:

Trust is the cornerstone of any successful business relationship. When you give freely, customers perceive your intentions as genuine and your expertise as authentic. This builds a solid foundation of trust, which is essential for long-term loyalty and engagement.

Generosity enables you to connect with your customers on a deeper, more meaningful level. By providing value without expectation, you demonstrate that you genuinely care about their needs and are invested in their success. This authenticity fosters strong relationships and customer loyalty.

When you go above and beyond in providing value, you surpass customer expectations. By offering more than what is typically anticipated, you create delightful experiences that leave a lasting impression. This sets you apart from your competitors and encourages customers to choose your brand over others.

Generosity has the power to generate positive word-of-mouth marketing. When customers experience exceptional value from your business, they are more likely to share their positive experiences with others. This organic promotion amplifies your brand's reach, attracting new customers who are drawn to the genuine value you provide.

A generous approach to business fosters deep customer loyalty. When customers feel appreciated, valued, and supported by your brand, they are more likely to remain loyal and continue engaging with your offerings. This loyalty translates into repeat business, positive referrals, and increased customer lifetime value.

In a crowded marketplace, generosity becomes a powerful differentiator. By giving freely, you set yourself apart from competitors who are solely focused on transactions. Customers perceive your brand as one that genuinely cares, values their needs, and goes the extra mile to provide value. This differentiation strengthens your brand's position and gives you a competitive edge.

Generosity creates a natural sense of reciprocity among customers. When you provide value without expectation, customers feel compelled to reciprocate by supporting your business in various ways. This can manifest as making purchases, engaging with your content, recommending your brand, or becoming brand ambassadors.

Generosity can turn customers into passionate advocates for your brand. When you consistently provide exceptional value, customers become not just satisfied customers but enthusiastic supporters. They willingly share their positive experiences, advocate for your brand, and become influential voices that attract new customers to your business.

Numerous businesses have thrived by embracing the power of generosity. From companies that offer free educational resources, trial periods, or complimentary services, to those that engage in social impact initiatives, these examples demonstrate that giving freely can be a catalyst for success.

As you embark on your journey to integrate generosity into your business strategy, keep in mind that it is not about empty gestures or superficial acts. True generosity stems from a genuine desire to make a positive impact and provide meaningful value. It requires a mindset shift, a commitment to prioritizing customer needs, and a willingness to go beyond conventional approaches.

When you harness the power of generosity, you have the opportunity to transform your business and create a lasting impact. Here are some actionable steps to embrace and implement the power of generosity in your business:

Take the time to deeply understand your customers' needs, challenges, and aspirations. This knowledge will guide you in identifying the areas where you can provide the most value and make a meaningful difference in their lives.

Assess your products, services, and resources to determine how you can offer value for free. Consider providing free resources such as e-books, webinars, or guides that address common customer pain points. Look for opportunities to offer complimentary consultations or trials to demonstrate the value you can bring.

Tailor your generosity to the specific needs of your customers. Make an effort to understand their unique circumstances and provide tailored solutions. This personalized approach enhances the perception of your brand's authenticity and care for individual customers.

To build trust and loyalty, consistently deliver value through your generous offerings. Whether it's regular blog posts, weekly newsletters, or ongoing free consultations, establish a cadence that allows your customers to rely on the consistent provision of valuable resources.

Create channels for customers to engage with your generosity initiatives. Encourage them to provide feedback, share their experiences, and suggest areas where they would appreciate further value. This feedback loop helps you continuously refine and improve your generosity strategy.

Explore opportunities for collaboration with like-minded individuals, organizations, or influencers. By pooling resources and knowledge, you can amplify the impact of your generosity and reach a wider audience. Collaborative efforts also enhance your credibility and expand your network.

Also, ensure that your customers are aware of the value you provide for free. Incorporate clear messaging and calls-to-action in your marketing materials, website, and social media platforms. Communicate the benefits and the impact that customers can expect from engaging with your generous offerings.

Measure impact and adjust. Track the impact of your generosity initiatives by monitoring metrics such as customer engagement, referrals, and customer lifetime value. Analyze the data to understand what is working well and where adjustments may be needed. Use these insights to refine your strategy and optimize your generosity efforts.

Remember, generosity is not about giving away everything indiscriminately or devaluing your products or services. It's about strategically providing value that aligns with your customers' needs while building trust, loyalty, and a strong brand reputation. When you embrace the power of generosity, you can create a business that not only thrives financially but also leaves a positive and lasting impact on your customers and community.

In the following chapters, we will delve deeper into the practical strategies and models for the concept of FREE.

Chapter 3

The Economics of Free

As a salesperson whether in the real estate sector or not, unlocking increased sales and revenue is very necessary. In this chapter, we will delve into the fascinating world of the economics of free, the underlying principles that make giving away products and services for free a viable and powerful strategy for increasing sales and revenue in your business. When you understand these, you will gain insights into how this seemingly counterintuitive approach can lead to significant financial gains.

The Value of Free: At first glance, giving away products or services for free may appear to undermine the traditional principles of economics. However, it is essential to recognize the hidden value in this approach. When you provide something of value for free, you can capture the attention, interest, and loyalty of potential customers who may have otherwise been hesitant to engage with your business.

The Power of Sampling: Offering free samples or trials allows customers to experience the value and quality of your products or services firsthand. This act of generosity creates a psychological reciprocity, as customers feel a sense of obligation to reciprocate the favor by making a purchase. Sampling acts as a powerful marketing tool, driving customer engagement and increasing the likelihood of future sales.

Building Trust and Credibility: Giving away something of value for free builds trust and credibility with your audience. When customers experience the quality and usefulness of your offerings, they develop confidence in your brand. This trust serves as a foundation for future transactions and encourages customers to become loyal advocates for your business.

Expanding Your Customer Base: Free offerings can act as a powerful magnet, attracting new customers who may have been reluctant to try your products or services otherwise. By removing the barriers to entry and providing a risk-free opportunity to engage with your business, you open the door to a broader audience. This expanded customer base provides a larger pool of potential customers who may eventually convert into paying customers.

Upselling and Cross-Selling Opportunities: The economics of free extends beyond the initial offering. Once you have gained the trust and attention of customers through your free products or services, you have the opportunity to upsell or cross-sell additional offerings. By demonstrating the value and quality of your free offering, customers become more willing to invest in related products or premium versions of what you provide.

Building Customer Lifetime Value: By adopting a long-term perspective, you recognize that the value of a customer extends beyond a single transaction. When you provide something for free, you invest in building a relationship with the customer, nurturing loyalty and repeat business. Customers who have benefited from your free offerings are more likely to become repeat customers, contributing to a higher customer lifetime value.

Harnessing the Power of Virality: Free offerings have the potential to go viral, spreading through word-of-mouth and social sharing. When customers experience exceptional value, they are motivated to share their positive experiences with others, leading to increased brand visibility and organic growth. This viral effect can amplify your reach and attract a wider audience, resulting in increased sales and revenue.

Creating a Competitive Advantage: In a crowded marketplace, the ability to offer something for free sets you apart from your competitors. It demonstrates your confidence in the value you provide and positions you as a customer-centric business. This competitive advantage can attract customers who value the opportunity to experience your offerings before committing to a purchase, giving you an edge in acquiring and retaining customers.

Data and Insights: Free offerings can provide valuable data and insights into customer preferences, behaviors, and needs. By analyzing the data generated from these interactions, you can make informed decisions about product development, marketing strategies, and customer segmentation. This data-driven approach enhances your ability to tailor your offerings and optimize your sales and revenue generation.

Monetization Strategies: While giving away products or services for free is a powerful strategy for increasing sales and revenue, it is crucial to develop effective monetization strategies that capitalize on the value created through generosity. Here are some key approaches to consider:

a. Freemium Model: Offer a basic version of your product or service for free, while charging for premium features or advanced functionality. This allows customers to experience the value you provide and motivates them to upgrade to a paid version for enhanced benefits.

b. Subscription Model: Provide a free trial period or limited access to your subscription-based service, enticing customers to subscribe for full access. The free offering serves as a gateway to acquiring long-term paying customers who recognize the value and benefits of your service.

c. Cross-promotion and Partnerships: Collaborate with complementary businesses to offer bundled products or services. By leveraging each other's customer base and combining offerings, you create a win-win situation where both businesses benefit from increased exposure and potential sales.

d. Advertising and Sponsorships: If you have a platform or a large audience, you can offer free content or services supported by advertising or sponsorships. By monetizing through third-party partnerships, you can continue to provide value for free while generating revenue from advertising or sponsored content.

e. Value-added Services or Upsells: While the core offering may be free, you can provide additional services, consulting, customization, or premium features at an added cost. This allows customers to tailor their experience and invest in the aspects that align with their specific needs or preferences.

f. Donations and Crowdfunding: For businesses that align with social causes or have a strong community focus, offering free products or services can be complemented by donation options or crowdfunding campaigns. This enables customers who value your free offerings to contribute voluntarily, supporting your mission and sustaining your business.

g. Data Monetization: If your free offerings generate valuable data, you can explore opportunities to monetize that data through partnerships or licensing agreements. By anonymizing and aggregating customer data, you can provide insights and analytics to other businesses, creating an additional revenue stream.

h. Upselling Support and Maintenance: For products or services that require ongoing support or maintenance, you can offer these services for a fee. While the core offering remains free, customers have the option to invest in professional assistance, updates, or technical support.

i. Limited-time Offers and Discounts: Use the free offering as a way to introduce customers to your brand and then provide time-limited discounts or exclusive offers to encourage them to make a purchase. This creates a sense of urgency and drives conversions.

j. Strategic Partnerships and Sponsorships: Seek opportunities to partner ith brands or organizations that align with your values and customer base. Through strategic partnerships and sponsorships, you can generate revenue while continuing to provide free offerings to your audience.

By implementing these monetization strategies effectively, you can capitalize on the value created through generosity and generate sustainable sales and revenue streams. It's important to strike a balance between providing free value and creating opportunities for customers to invest in premium offerings or additional services that enhance their experience.

In the upcoming chapters, we will explore these monetization strategies in more detail, providing practical examples and insights to help you navigate the complex landscape of generating revenue while maintaining the spirit of generosity in your business.

Chapter 4

The Psychology of Free

In this chapter, we will delve into the fascinating realm of the psychology of free and explore how this concept triggers a powerful psychological response in customers. Understanding the underlying psychological factors can help you effectively leverage the concept of free to attract and retain customers. Let's explore some key psychological principles at play:

Perceived Value: The concept of free carries an inherent psychological value. When customers see something offered for free, it triggers a perception of high value and opportunity. They feel they are getting something of worth without any monetary cost, leading to a positive emotional response and increased interest in the offering.

Reciprocity: The principle of reciprocity plays a significant role in the psychology of free. When you provide something of value for free, customers feel a sense of indebtedness and a desire to reciprocate the gesture. This reciprocity can manifest as increased brand loyalty, word-of-mouth referrals, or even future purchases.

Loss Aversion: Humans have a natural aversion to loss. When customers perceive something as free, they fear missing out on the opportunity and experiencing a loss if they don't take advantage of it. This fear of missing out drives customers to engage with the free offering, creating a sense of urgency and motivation to act.

Trust and Relationship Building: Offering something for free establishes trust and fosters a positive relationship with customers. When customers experience the value you provide without any upfront commitment, it builds trust in your brand and strengthens the customer-business relationship. This foundation of trust becomes instrumental in future interactions and potential sales.

Anchoring Effect: The psychology of free can be used as an anchor point for customers' perception of value. By initially offering something for free, you establish a reference point from which customers evaluate the value of your other offerings. When customers perceive the free offering as valuable, it positively influences their perception of the paid offerings, making them more likely to make a purchase.

Experiential Sampling: Providing free samples or trials allows customers to experience your products or services firsthand. This experiential sampling taps into the psychological principle of "try before you buy," reducing perceived risk and uncertainty. It enables customers to assess the quality, benefits, and fit of your offerings, increasing the likelihood of future conversions.

Social Proof and Social Influence: When customers see others benefiting from your free offerings, it triggers the psychological principle of social proof. Social proof acts as a powerful influencer, as people tend to follow the behavior and choices of others. By showcasing positive testimonials, reviews, or social media endorsements of your free offerings, you can leverage the power of social influence to attract and retain customers.

Cognitive Dissonance: Providing something for free can create cognitive dissonance in customers' minds. They may question why you are giving away something valuable without any cost. This cognitive dissonance motivates customers to reconcile the perceived inconsistency by engaging further with your business, such as making a purchase or recommending your brand to others.

Habit Formation: Free offerings can serve as a catalyst for habit formation. When customers engage with your free offerings and derive value from them, it creates a habit of seeking out and relying on your brand for their needs. This habit formation leads to increased customer retention, repeat purchases, and long-term loyalty.

Emotional Connection: The psychology of free taps into customers' emotions, creating a positive emotional connection with your brand. When customers feel they have received something valuable without expecting it, it evokes feelings of gratitude, happiness, and satisfaction. This emotional connection strengthens their affinity for your brand and fuels their desire to engage further.

Harnessing The Power Of Customer Psychology

When you understand and leverage the psychology of free, you can strategically design your offerings, marketing messages, and customer interactions to maximize their impact. Here are some practical strategies to achieve this:

a. Highlighting Value: Emphasize the value customers will receive from your free offering. Clearly communicate the benefits, features, and unique selling points that make it valuable. This helps customers perceive the free offering as something worthwhile and increases their motivation to engage with it.

b. Limited Availability: Create a sense of scarcity and exclusivity around your free offering. By setting limits on the availability or time frame of the free offer, you tap into customers' fear of missing out. This motivates them to take immediate action and increases their appreciation for the opportunity.

c. Social Proof: Leverage the power of social proof by showcasing testimonials, case studies, or user-generated content that highlight the positive experiences of customers who have benefited from your free offering. This social validation enhances credibility, builds trust, and encourages others to follow suit.

d. Clear Call-to-Action: Provide a clear and compelling call-to-action that directs customers on how to engage with your free offering. Whether it's signing up for a trial, downloading a free guide, or attending a webinar, guide customers through the process and make it easy for them to take the next step.

e. Personalization: Tailor your free offering to the specific needs and preferences of your target audience. The more personalized and relevant the offer is, the stronger the psychological impact. Customization creates a sense of exclusivity and makes customers feel seen and understood.

f. Upsell and Cross-sell Opportunities: Once customers have engaged with your free offering, seize the opportunity to present them with relevant upsell or cross-sell options. Capitalize on their positive experience by showcasing how the paid products or services can further enhance their benefits and address their specific needs.

g. Transparent Value Exchange: Clearly communicate the value exchange customers can expect. While the offering is free, let customers know how you will derive value, such as through their feedback, data collection, or the potential for future purchases. Transparency builds trust and establishes a mutually beneficial relationship.

h. Continuous Engagement: Use the free offering as a starting point for ongoing engagement. Provide additional resources, content, or educational materials to keep customers connected and interested in your brand. Nurture the relationship and build loyalty over time.

i. Emotional Appeal: Appeal to customers' emotions by sharing stories, testimonials, or experiences that evoke positive feelings. Connect with their aspirations, desires, or pain points, and demonstrate how your free offering can positively impact their lives or businesses. Emotional resonance increases engagement and creates a lasting impression.

j. Seek Feedback: Use customer feedback and

insights gathered through the free offering to refine and improve your paid offerings. Actively seek feedback, listen to customer suggestions, and iterate based on their needs. This not only enhances the value you provide but also demonstrates your commitment to customer satisfaction.

Chapter 5
Creating a Free Offer That Converts

The concept behind creating a free offer that converts as a realtor or even a business person is that you begin to create irresistible value propositions. In this chapter, we will look at the art of creating a free offer that not only captures the attention of prospective clients but also converts them into leads and drives sales.

Developing an irresistible value proposition is key to enticing potential customers to engage with your free offer and ultimately take the desired action. Here are some tips and techniques for crafting an offer that generates leads and drives sales:

Understand Your Target Audience: Begin by gaining a deep understanding of your target audience. What are their pain points, desires, and aspirations? What solutions are they seeking? By understanding your audience's needs, you can tailor your free offer to provide valuable solutions that resonate with them.

Offer High Perceived Value: Your free offer should provide significant value to your target audience. It should be something they perceive as valuable, helpful, and relevant to their needs. The more value they perceive in your offer, the more motivated they will be to engage with it and take the next step in their customer journey.

Solve a Specific Problem: Identify a specific problem or challenge that your target audience faces, and design your free offer to address it. By focusing on a specific problem, you position yourself as an expert in that area and demonstrate your ability to provide effective solutions. This targeted approach increases the likelihood of attracting qualified leads.

Showcase Results and Benefits: Clearly communicate the results and benefits that customers can expect from your free offer. Highlight the positive outcomes they can achieve by engaging with your offer. Whether it's saving time, increasing productivity, improving skills, or achieving a specific goal, paint a vivid picture of the benefits they will experience.

Provide Actionable Content: Make sure your free offer provides actionable content that your audience can immediately implement and see results. Whether it's a guide, checklist, template, tutorial, or webinar, ensure that it offers practical steps or insights that your audience can apply to their specific situation. This actionable content builds trust and positions you as a valuable resource.

Create a Sense of Urgency: To prompt immediate action, create a sense of urgency around your free offer. Set a limited time frame, use words like "limited availability" or "exclusive offer," or provide a bonus incentive for early adopters. This urgency motivates prospective clients to take action before the opportunity passes, increasing conversions.

Use Persuasive Copywriting: Craft compelling and persuasive copy that clearly communicates the value of your free offer. Focus on addressing your audience's pain points, using persuasive language, and emphasizing the benefits they will gain. Use storytelling techniques, social proof, and testimonials to engage your audience and build trust.

Optimize Landing Pages: Design a dedicated landing page that is focused solely on promoting your free offer. Optimize the page with persuasive copy, attention-grabbing headlines, clear calls-to-action, and visually appealing graphics. Keep the page clean, easy to navigate, and free from distractions to maximize conversions.

Implement Lead Capture Mechanisms: Integrate lead capture mechanisms into your free offer to collect valuable contact information from prospective clients. This allows you to continue nurturing the relationship and converting leads into paying customers over time. Use opt-in forms, email subscriptions, or gated content to capture leads effectively.

Test, Rinse, Repeat: Continuously test and refine your free offer to optimize its performance. Collect data, analyze the results, and make adjustments as necessary to improve the offer's effectiveness and drive better results.

With these, you can create a free offer that captures the attention of prospective clients and converts them into leads and sales. To align your offer with your overall business objectives and customer journey, pay attention to these:

Segment Your Offers: Tailor your free offers to different segments of your target audience. Consider creating multiple offers that cater to various customer needs, preferences, or stages of the buying cycle. This allows you to attract a wider range of prospects and increase the chances of conversion.

Leverage Social Proof: Incorporate social proof elements into your free offer to build credibility and trust. Include testimonials, success stories, or case studies that highlight the positive experiences of previous customers who have benefited from your offer. This social validation strengthens your value proposition and encourages others to take action.

Use Engaging Multimedia: Enhance the appeal of your

free offer by incorporating engaging multimedia elements such as videos, infographics, or interactive content. Visual and interactive elements capture attention, increase retention, and provide a more immersive experience for your audience.

Promote Sharing and Referrals: Encourage recipients of your free offer to share it with others and refer their friends or colleagues. Implement referral programs or provide incentives for sharing, such as exclusive bonuses or discounts. This amplifies the reach of your offer and generates additional leads through word-of-mouth marketing.

Follow Up and Nurture Leads: Once prospects have engaged with your free offer, it's essential to follow up and nurture those leads. Implement a systematic approach to lead nurturing through email marketing, personalized communications, or targeted content. Continue to provide value and build a relationship with your leads, gradually guiding them towards a purchase decision.

Remember, creating a free offer that converts requires a deep understanding of your target audience, a compelling value proposition, and strategic implementation. With a well-crafted free offer, you can capture the attention of prospective clients, generate leads, and drive sales, ultimately growing your business and achieving your goals.

Chapter 6
Building Trust Through Free Content

If you desire to establish expertise and foster customer loyalty, you can leverage the power of content to achieve these. When you share valuable content without expecting anything in return, you establish yourself as an expert in your field and foster long-term customer loyalty.

Here are some strategies for creating valuable content that not only educates and engages your audience but also builds trust and credibility:

Understand Your Audience's Needs: To create content that resonates with your audience, you must first understand their needs, pain points, and aspirations. Conduct thorough research, engage with your target audience through surveys or interviews, and listen to their feedback. This insight will help you tailor your content to address their specific challenges and provide valuable solutions.

Provide Actionable Insights: Create content that offers practical and actionable insights your audience can implement in their lives or businesses. Whether it's a blog post, a video tutorial, a podcast episode, or an infographic, ensure that your content provides tangible value and leaves your audience with actionable takeaways. This positions you as a trusted source of expertise and establishes your credibility.

Showcase Your Knowledge and Expertise: Share your knowledge and expertise freely through your content. Demonstrate your understanding of the subject matter, provide in-depth analysis, and offer unique perspectives. By showcasing your expertise, you build trust and credibility with your audience, positioning yourself as a go-to resource in your industry or niche.

Be Transparent and Authentic: Be transparent and authentic in your content. Share personal anecdotes, lessons learned, and real-life experiences that relate to your audience's challenges. Authenticity helps your audience relate to you on a deeper level and fosters a genuine connection. Avoid excessive self-promotion and focus on delivering value instead.

Educate and Empower: Use your free content to educate and empower your audience. Provide them with the knowledge and tools they need to make informed decisions or take specific actions. The more you empower your audience, the more they will trust your expertise and rely on you for guidance.

Consistency and Quality: Consistency is key in building trust through content. Develop a consistent publishing schedule and deliver content of high quality on a regular basis. This demonstrates your commitment to providing value and builds trust by showing that you are reliable and dependable.

Engage and Respond: Encourage audience engagement by inviting comments, questions, and feedback on your content. Respond promptly and thoughtfully to their inquiries, showing that you value their input and are genuinely interested in their success. This two-way communication strengthens the trust and connection between you and your audience.

Leverage Different Formats: Vary the format of your free content to cater to different learning preferences and consumption habits. Some people prefer reading blog posts, while others enjoy watching videos or listening to podcasts. By offering content in different formats, you can reach a broader audience and provide value in a way that resonates with them.

Utilize Case Studies and Success Stories: Incorporate case studies and success stories into your content to demonstrate real-world examples of how your expertise has helped others. Highlight the challenges faced, the strategies implemented, and the positive outcomes achieved. These stories serve as social proof and further enhance your credibility.

Personalize Your Content: Tailor your content to address specific segments or personas within your target audience. Personalization creates a sense of relevance and demonstrates that you understand your audience's unique needs and preferences. Whether through targeted blog posts, customized newsletters, or segmented email campaigns, personalize your content to establish a deeper connection with your audience.

Collaborate and Guest Authorship: Seek opportunities to collaborate with other experts or industry influencers. This can involve guest authoring on their platforms, contributing to collaborative projects, or participating in interviews or panel discussions. Collaborative efforts enhance your credibility by association and expose your content to new audiences, expanding your reach and building trust.

Offer Exclusive Content or Resources: Create special content or resources that are exclusively available to your audience. This could be in the form of e-books, whitepapers, templates, or premium video content. By providing exclusive content, you show your audience that you value their support and are willing to go the extra mile to provide them with valuable resources.

Share Testimonials and Social Proof: Incorporate testimonials and social proof into your content to reinforce trust and credibility. Showcase positive feedback and success stories from satisfied customers or clients. Testimonials provide evidence of the value you deliver and the positive impact you have on others, further establishing your expertise.

Stay Up to Date and Relevant: Continuously stay informed about the latest trends, developments, and insights in your industry. Share up-to-date and relevant information with your audience through your content. This demonstrates that you are actively engaged in your field and are committed to delivering the most current and valuable information.

Measure and Analyze Results: Regularly measure and analyze the performance of your content to assess its impact and effectiveness. Track metrics such as engagement levels, social shares, website traffic, and conversions. By understanding what resonates with your audience and what drives results, you can refine your content strategy to continually improve and provide even greater value.

If you implement these strategies for creating valuable content, you can build trust and credibility with your audience. Your free content becomes a vehicle for establishing yourself as an expert, fostering customer loyalty, and ultimately driving business growth. Remember, delivering consistent, high-quality content that addresses your audience's needs and empowers them is the key to building trust and creating lasting relationships.

Chapter 7
Leveraging the Power of
Social Media

Social media has revolutionized the way we connect and share information, providing an unprecedented opportunity to promote your free content, build trust, and drive meaningful engagement. Anyone can leverage the power of social media to maximize the impact of their free offerings. To start, you must pay attention to these:

Choose the Right Platforms: Start by identifying the social media platforms that align best with your target audience and business objectives. Each platform has its unique characteristics and user demographics. Whether it's Facebook, Instagram, Twitter, LinkedIn, YouTube, or others, select the platforms where your audience is most active and receptive to the type of content you offer.

Define Your Social Media Strategy: Develop a clear social media strategy that aligns with your overall marketing goals and free offerings. Determine the key messages you want to convey, the tone of voice, and the types of content you will share. Establish specific objectives, such as increasing brand awareness, driving website traffic, generating leads, or fostering community engagement.

Promote Your Free Offerings: Use social media as a powerful promotional tool for your free offerings. Create attention-grabbing posts, videos, or graphics that highlight the value and benefits of your free content. Incorporate persuasive copy, compelling visuals, and clear calls-to-action to encourage your audience to engage with and share your offerings.

Create Engaging Content: Social media thrives on engaging and shareable content. Develop a variety of content formats, such as blog posts, videos, infographics, live streams, or interactive polls, that resonate with your audience. Deliver content that educates, entertains, inspires, or solves problems, sparking conversations and encouraging your followers to interact with your brand.

Foster Community Engagement: Cultivate an active and engaged community around your brand by encouraging interaction and dialogue on social media. Respond promptly to comments, messages, and inquiries from your followers. Initiate conversations, ask thought-provoking questions, and encourage user-generated content. Actively engage with your audience to build relationships and foster a sense of belonging.

Share Valuable Insights and Tips: Provide regular doses of valuable content on social media. Share insights, tips, industry news, or relevant resources that align with your expertise and audience's interests. Position yourself as a trusted source of information and go-to expert in your field. By consistently providing value, you establish credibility and encourage followers to seek out your free offerings.

Utilize Hashtags and Trending Topics: Leverage hashtags and trending topics to expand the visibility of your free offerings. Research popular hashtags and incorporate them into your posts to reach a wider audience. Monitor industry trends and participate in relevant conversations to position your brand at the forefront of discussions. This increases the chances of your content being discovered and shared.

Collaborate with Influencers and Partners: Collaborate with influencers, industry experts, or complementary brands to amplify the reach of your free offerings. Partner with individuals or organizations that have a significant following and align with your brand values. Co-create content, host joint webinars or live events, or engage in cross-promotion to tap into their audience and expand your reach.

Encourage User-generated Content: Encourage your followers to create and share their own content related to your free offerings. Run contests, challenges, or campaigns that prompt users to share their experiences, testimonials, or creative interpretations of your content. User-generated content not only generates buzz but also serves as powerful social proof, fostering authenticity and trust.

Build Relationships with Influencers: Cultivate relationships with influencers in your industry or niche. Engage with their content, share their insights, and establish meaningful connections. By building relationships with influencers, you can leverage their credibility and reach to amplify the visibility of your free offerings. Collaborate on content, seek endorsements, or invite them to participate in webinars or interviews.

Harness the Power of Social Ads: Consider investing in social media advertising to extend the reach of your free offerings. Target specific demographics, interests, or behaviors to ensure that your content reaches the right audience. Use compelling ad copy, visually appealing graphics, and clear calls-to-action to entice users to engage with your free offerings.

Monitor and Respond to Feedback: Actively monitor social media for feedback, reviews, or mentions related to your free offerings. Respond promptly and professionally to both positive and negative feedback. Address concerns, provide additional support, and show your willingness to listen and improve. Engaging with your audience's feedback demonstrates your commitment to their satisfaction and builds trust.

Encourage Social Sharing: Make it easy for your audience to share your free offerings on social media. Incorporate social sharing buttons or widgets on your website, blog, or landing pages. Encourage your audience to share their experiences with your content and incentivize them to spread the word. The more your free offerings are shared, the wider their reach and impact.

Measure Return on Investment (ROI): Assess the return on investment of your social media efforts in relation to your free offerings. Track the number of leads generated, conversions, website traffic, and the overall impact on your business objectives. By measuring ROI, you can allocate resources effectively and optimize your social media strategy for maximum results.

When you leverage the power of social media, you can significantly amplify the reach of your free offerings, build a thriving community of engaged followers, and drive meaningful engagement. Social media platforms provide an unprecedented opportunity to connect with your target audience, showcase your expertise, and foster a sense of trust and loyalty. Embrace the potential of social media as a strategic tool in your free offerings' promotion, and unlock its power to drive your business forward.

Chapter 8

The Art of Monetizing Free

While the concept of giving away everything for free may seem counterintuitive to traditional business models, it opens up new avenues for revenue generation and long-term sustainability. Here are different monetization models that can be applied to free offerings while maintaining the spirit of generosity:

Freemium Model: The freemium model offers a basic version of your product or service for free, while charging for premium features or advanced functionality. This model allows you to capture a large user base through your free offering, while enticing a portion of them to upgrade to a paid version. By providing value upfront, you build trust and showcase the value of your offering, increasing the likelihood of conversions.

Upselling and Cross-selling: Use your free offerings as a platform to upsell or cross-sell complementary products or services. Once your audience experiences the value of your free content, they may be more inclined to invest in additional offerings that enhance their experience or provide added benefits. For example, if you offer free training videos, you can upsell premium courses or coaching services.

Affiliate Marketing: Incorporate affiliate marketing into your free offerings by promoting relevant products or services from other businesses. By recommending high-quality offerings to your audience, you can earn a commission on any resulting sales. Choose affiliate partnerships carefully, ensuring that the products align with your audience's needs and maintain your reputation for providing valuable recommendations.

Sponsored Content and Collaborations: Collaborate with brands or businesses to create sponsored content related to your free offerings. This can involve writing sponsored blog posts, hosting sponsored webinars, or featuring sponsored videos. However, ensure that any sponsored content is transparent and clearly labeled as such to maintain transparency and authenticity.

Advertising Revenue: Generate revenue by incorporating targeted advertising into your free offerings. Display relevant ads on your website, blog, or within your free content. Platforms like YouTube allow content creators to monetize their videos through ads. However, be mindful of balancing user experience with advertising and ensure that the ads do not overwhelm or detract from the value you provide.

Premium Membership or Subscription: Create a

premium membership or subscription model that provides exclusive benefits or access to additional content or resources. Offer enhanced features, personalized support, or advanced training to members who pay a recurring fee. This model incentivizes your audience to become paying members while still allowing others to access valuable free content.

Donations and Crowdfunding: Give your audience the option to support your free offerings through voluntary donations or crowdfunding. Set up a system where users can contribute funds as a gesture of appreciation for the value they receive. This approach relies on the goodwill of your audience and emphasizes the importance of community support.

Licensing or Reselling: Explore opportunities to license or resell your free content to other businesses or platforms. This could involve selling the rights to use your content in training programs, publications, or digital products. By monetizing the usage of your content, you can generate revenue while expanding its reach and impact.

Consultancy or Coaching Services: Position yourself as an expert in your field and offer consultancy or coaching services based on your free offerings. Once your audience recognizes your expertise and trusts your knowledge, they may seek personalized guidance or assistance in implementing the insights you provide. This allows you to monetize your expertise and provide tailored solutions to clients.

Product or Merchandise Sales: Develop products or merchandise related to your free offerings and sell them to your audience. This could include physical products, digital downloads, or branded merchandise. By creating tangible products that align with the value you provide in your free offerings, you can cater to the needs and preferences of your audience while generating additional revenue.

Events and Workshops: Organize live events, workshops, or conferences centered around your free offerings. Offer tickets or registrations at a fee, providing attendees with immersive experiences, networking opportunities, and exclusive access to expert insights. Events can be a powerful revenue-generating avenue while bringing your community together and fostering meaningful connections.

Sponsored Partnerships: Seek out sponsored partnerships with businesses that align with your brand values and audience interests. Collaborate on joint initiatives, such as co-creating content, hosting webinars, or launching promotional campaigns. By leveraging the resources and reach of your partners, you can monetize your free offerings while expanding your audience and creating mutually beneficial relationships.

Licensing Intellectual Property: If you have developed valuable intellectual property through your free offerings, consider licensing it to other organizations or individuals. This can involve granting rights to use your content, software, or patented technologies in exchange for licensing fees. Licensing allows you to monetize your intellectual assets while leveraging the expertise and distribution networks of other entities.

Sponsored Newsletter or Subscriptions: If you have a newsletter or subscription-based content, explore the option of sponsored placements or partnerships. Allow relevant businesses to advertise or contribute sponsored content within your newsletters or subscription-based offerings. This not only diversifies your revenue streams but also provides additional exposure and value to your audience.

Customization and Personalization: Offer

customization or personalized services related to your free offerings for a fee. Provide tailored solutions, advice, or recommendations that cater to the specific needs and preferences of individual customers. By offering personalized experiences, you can command premium pricing and generate revenue while delivering exceptional value.

It's important to strike a balance between generating revenue and maintaining the spirit of generosity that underlies your free offerings. Always prioritize the value you provide to your audience and ensure that any monetization strategies align with their interests and needs. Transparency and authenticity are key in building trust and loyalty, so be upfront about your monetization methods and the value they bring.

Remember, the art of monetizing free lies in finding creative ways to generate revenue while continuing to deliver exceptional value and nurturing your community. Embrace a holistic approach that combines various monetization models, tailoring them to your specific audience and business context. By doing so, you can sustainably monetize your free offerings while staying true to your ethos of generosity and building a thriving and profitable business.

Chapter 9

Cultivating Relationships
with Free Customers

As a salesperson, you need to learn how to turn fans into loyal advocates after attracting a community of free customers who have engaged with your offerings and experienced the value you provide. The deal is to get these free customers, and turn them into loyal advocates who not only support your business but also become valuable sources of referrals and repeat business. Let's dive into the key strategies for nurturing these relationships:

Personalized Communication: Treat your free customers as individuals by personalizing your communication with them. Address them by name, acknowledge their engagement with your free offerings, and tailor your messaging to their specific interests and needs. Use email marketing, social media interactions, or personalized messaging platforms to deliver targeted and relevant content that deepens their connection with your brand.

Exclusive Benefits and Rewards: Create exclusive benefits or rewards for your free customers to make them feel valued and appreciated. Offer them early access to new content, exclusive discounts, or special promotions. By providing additional value beyond the free offerings, you incentivize their continued engagement and foster a sense of loyalty.

Upselling and Cross-selling: Strategically introduce upselling and cross-selling opportunities to your free customers. Identify complementary products or services that align with their needs and interests and offer them as valuable extensions of the free offerings they have already experienced. Showcase the additional benefits and value they can gain by investing in these offerings, making it a natural progression in their journey with your brand.

Remarketing and Retargeting: Implement remarketing and retargeting techniques to stay on the radar of your free customers. Use website pixels or email marketing tools to track their interactions and behavior. Then, deliver targeted ads, emails, or content that remind them of the value they received and encourage them to take the next step in their engagement with your brand.

Customer Feedback and Surveys: Actively seek feedback from your free customers to understand their preferences, challenges, and aspirations. Use surveys, polls, or feedback forms to gather insights that can inform your product or service development. This not only shows that you value their opinions but also enables you to enhance your offerings based on their needs, increasing their likelihood of conversion and repeat business.

Community Building: Foster a sense of community among your free customers by creating platforms for interaction and collaboration. Establish online forums, social media groups, or dedicated communities where they can connect, share experiences, and support one another. Actively participate in these communities, provide guidance, and encourage discussions to build a strong sense of belonging and loyalty.

Exceptional Customer Support: Provide exceptional customer support to your free customers, addressing their inquiries, concerns, or issues promptly and professionally. Offer multiple channels of communication, such as email, live chat, or phone support, and ensure that their experience with your brand is positive and hassle-free. By delivering outstanding support, you demonstrate your commitment to their success and cultivate long-term loyalty.

Valuable Content and Resources: Continue to deliver valuable content and resources to your free customers, even after their initial engagement. Share relevant blog posts, tutorials, case studies, or industry insights that align with their interests and needs. By consistently providing value, you position yourself as a trusted source of expertise and reinforce their decision to engage with your brand.

Referral Programs: Encourage your free customers to become advocates for your brand by implementing a referral program. Offer incentives, discounts, or exclusive rewards to those who refer new customers or promote your offerings. Word-of-mouth recommendations from satisfied customers are highly influential and can drive substantial growth and conversions.

Relationship Building Events: Organize events or webinars specifically designed to deepen your relationships with free customers. Provide opportunities for them to interact with you, ask questions, and gain further insights. These events also serve as a platform for building a sense of community among your free customers, allowing them to connect with like-minded individuals and share their experiences.

Loyalty Programs: Implement a loyalty program tailored to your free customers. Reward them for their continued engagement, such as by offering points, tiers, or exclusive perks based on their level of involvement with your brand. This encourages them to stay loyal and actively participate in your offerings, increasing the likelihood of repeat business.

Personalized Recommendations: Leverage the data and insights you have gathered about your free customers to provide personalized recommendations. Use algorithms or AI-powered systems to suggest relevant products, services, or content based on their past interactions and preferences. By delivering tailored recommendations, you enhance their experience and demonstrate that you understand their individual needs.

Surprises and Delightful Moments: Create memorable experiences for your free customers by surprising them with unexpected gestures or rewards. This could involve sending personalized thank-you notes, offering exclusive access to limited-time offers, or providing unexpected bonuses. These delightful moments not only enhance their perception of your brand but also deepen their emotional connection, fostering long-term loyalty.

Thought Leadership and Expertise: Establish yourself as a thought leader in your industry and share your expertise with your free customers. Publish insightful articles, deliver webinars or podcasts, or speak at relevant events to showcase your knowledge and provide valuable insights. By positioning yourself as an authority, you build trust and credibility, making your free customers more likely to convert and become loyal advocates.

Continuous Improvement and Innovation: Strive for continuous improvement and innovation in your free offerings. Regularly assess and enhance the value you provide, based on customer feedback and market trends. This demonstrates your commitment to delivering the best possible experience and encourages your free customers to stay engaged and explore new opportunities with your brand.

Remember, cultivating relationships with your free customers requires ongoing effort and genuine care. Treat them with respect, listen to their feedback, and consistently deliver value. By nurturing these relationships, you not only increase the likelihood of upselling and cross-selling opportunities but also create a loyal community of advocates who will spread the word about your brand and contribute to its long-term success.

Chapter 10
Overcoming the Fear of Competition

Now, let's tackle the common fears and misconceptions surrounding competition and explore the abundance mindset that can transform your perspective as a salesperson. It's natural to feel apprehensive about competition, but by shifting your mindset and embracing collaboration, you can unlock new opportunities for growth and success.

Acknowledge the Source of Fear. Start by recognizing that the fear of competition often stems from a scarcity mindset, the belief that there is limited market share or resources to go around. Understand that this mindset is based on a false premise and can hinder your progress.

Instead, adopt an abundance mindset that focuses on the vast opportunities available and the potential for collaboration.

Embrace Healthy Competition. Rather than viewing competition as a threat, reframe it as a positive force that drives innovation and pushes you to deliver better products or services. Healthy competition can inspire you to elevate your offerings, differentiate your brand, and continually improve. Embrace the challenge and use it as motivation to excel.

Shift to a Collaboration Mindset. Recognize that collaboration can be more powerful than competition. Instead of viewing other businesses as rivals, seek opportunities for partnerships, joint ventures, or collaborations. By leveraging each other's strengths and resources, you can create win-win situations that benefit all parties involved. Collaboration fosters innovation, expands your network, and opens doors to new markets.

Focus on Your Unique Value Proposition. Rather than fixating on what your competitors are doing, concentrate on developing and showcasing your unique value proposition. Identify your strengths, unique selling points, and the specific value you bring to your customers. By focusing on your distinctive qualities, you create a niche that sets you apart from the competition.

Embrace Customer-Centricity. Prioritize understanding and meeting the needs of your customers. By truly listening to their feedback and preferences, you can tailor your offerings to provide exceptional value. By putting your customers at the center of your business, you build strong relationships and loyalty that can withstand competition.

Learn from Competitors. Instead of fearing

competitors, view them as a source of learning and inspiration. Study their strategies, observe their successes and failures, and identify areas where you can improve or differentiate. By analyzing the competition, you gain valuable insights that can inform your own business decisions and foster innovation.

Collaborative Marketing Efforts. Explore opportunities for collaborative marketing efforts with complementary businesses. Partnering with others in your industry or related sectors can expand your reach and attract new customers. Joint promotions, co-marketing campaigns, or cross-referencing can create a win-win situation by pooling resources and leveraging each other's customer base.

Network and Build Relationships. Engage in industry events, conferences, and networking opportunities to connect with fellow professionals and potential collaborators. Building strong relationships within your industry can lead to partnerships, referrals, and mutually beneficial collaborations. Attend events, join professional organizations, and actively participate in relevant communities to expand your network.

Focus on Continuous Improvement. Rather than obsessing over your competitors, prioritize your own growth and continuous improvement. Invest in your skills, knowledge, and processes to stay ahead of the game. By constantly innovating and striving for excellence, you position yourself as a leader in your field, making competition less intimidating.

Trust in Your Unique Journey. Remind yourself that your business has its unique journey and purpose. Trust in your vision, values, and the value you bring to your customers. Your authenticity and commitment to delivering exceptional experiences will attract customers who resonate with your brand, irrespective of the competition.

Remember, competition is an inherent part of any business landscape. Instead of fearing it, embrace it as a catalyst for growth and collaboration. By shifting your mindset to one of abundance and adopting a collaborative approach, you can transform competition into an opportunity for mutual success. Embrace the following strategies to overcome the fear of competition and thrive in your industry:

Foster a Supportive Community. Surround yourself with like-minded entrepreneurs and professionals who share a collaborative mindset. Join industry-specific groups, attend conferences, or participate in mastermind sessions where you can connect with peers who understand the value of collaboration over competition. Building a supportive community allows you to share insights, exchange ideas, and even collaborate on projects that benefit everyone involved.

Seek Strategic Partnerships. Identify businesses or

individuals in your industry or related sectors who can complement your offerings. Look for opportunities to form strategic partnerships that align with your goals and values. By pooling resources, expertise, and networks, you can create powerful collaborations that expand your reach and deliver more value to your customers.

Joint Ventures and Co-creation. Consider joint ventures or co-creation initiatives with competitors or businesses in related fields. By combining your strengths, you can create innovative products, services, or experiences that cater to a broader audience. These ventures allow you to tap into new markets, access new distribution channels, and leverage shared expertise, ultimately benefiting all parties involved.

Share Knowledge and Resources. Embrace the philosophy of sharing knowledge and resources within your industry. Instead of hoarding information, be open to sharing insights, best practices, and experiences with others. This fosters a collaborative environment where everyone can learn and grow together. By freely sharing your expertise, you establish yourself as a trusted authority and build strong relationships with peers and potential collaborators.

Collaborative Marketing Campaigns. Explore opportunities for collaborative marketing campaigns with businesses that target similar audiences. By combining your resources and marketing efforts, you can amplify your reach and create more impactful campaigns. Joint webinars, guest blogging, co-hosted events, or even co-branded products can help you tap into new markets and attract a wider customer base.

Referrals and Partnerships. Develop referral networks with complementary businesses. Identify non-competitive companies that serve a similar customer base and establish referral agreements. By referring customers to each other, you provide added value and build trust. This mutually beneficial approach helps you expand your customer reach while delivering a seamless experience to your audience.

Emphasize Collaboration in Brand Messaging. Infuse the spirit of collaboration into your brand messaging and communication. Highlight the value you place on partnerships, teamwork, and collective growth. By positioning your brand as one that embraces collaboration, you attract like-minded customers who appreciate and support your collaborative approach.

Learn from Competitors. Rather than viewing competitors as threats, view them as sources of inspiration and learning. Study their successes and failures, analyze their strategies, and adapt relevant insights to your own business. Embrace a mindset of continuous improvement, using competition as a motivator to innovate and deliver even better experiences to your customers.

Focus on Unique Differentiators. Instead of fixating on what your competitors are doing, focus on what makes your business unique. Identify your strengths, unique selling points, and distinctive value proposition. Communicate these differentiators clearly to your target audience, emphasizing how your offerings stand out in the market. By highlighting your unique qualities, you can attract customers who resonate with your brand and are less swayed by the presence of competition.

Collaborative Problem-Solving. Engage in collaborative problem-solving within your industry. Participate in forums, conferences, or online communities where industry professionals come together to address common challenges. By actively contributing to these discussions and collaborating on finding solutions, you not only build relationships but also contribute to the overall growth and improvement of your industry.

Remember, competition should not be seen as a barrier but as an opportunity for growth and collaboration. When you overcome the fear of competition and embrace a collaborative mindset, you position yourself for long-term success in your industry. To achieve this, you should:

Celebrate Healthy Competition: Instead of viewing competition as a threat, see it as a sign of a thriving market. Healthy competition indicates that there is a demand for your products or services. Embrace it as a motivator to push yourself further, innovate, and continually improve your offerings.

Focus on Customer Value: Keep your focus on delivering exceptional value to your customers. When you prioritize their needs and exceed their expectations, you build a loyal customer base that remains loyal even in the presence of competition. Emphasize the unique benefits and advantages you offer, ensuring that your customers see the value in choosing your business over others.

Collaborate for Innovation: Collaboration can lead to innovation and breakthroughs. Seek out opportunities to collaborate with competitors, industry experts, or even customers. By pooling resources, knowledge, and perspectives, you can tackle industry challenges, develop innovative solutions, and create a positive impact within your market.

Seek Inspiration, Not Comparison: Instead of comparing yourself constantly to competitors, use them as a source of inspiration. Look at their successes and strategies to glean insights that you can adapt to your own business. Focus on your own journey, setting your goals and benchmarks for success.

Embrace Coopetition: Coopetition refers to the concept of cooperating with competitors for mutual benefit. Identify areas where collaboration can be mutually advantageous, such as sharing resources, joint marketing initiatives, or even cross-referrals. By working together strategically, you can create a win-win situation that benefits both parties.

Build Strategic Alliances: Form strategic alliances with businesses that complement your offerings but don't directly compete with you. These alliances can open doors to new markets, expand your reach, and create a network of support. Look for partners who share similar values and target similar customer segments.

Focus on Continuous Learning: Commit yourself to continuous learning and improvement. Stay informed about industry trends, technological advancements, and evolving customer preferences. This knowledge will help you adapt, stay ahead of the competition, and identify new opportunities for growth.

Engage in Collaboration Platforms: Join online platforms or communities that foster collaboration within your industry. These platforms provide opportunities to connect with professionals, share insights, and collaborate on projects. By actively participating in these communities, you expand your network and stay connected with industry developments.

Develop Your Unique Brand: Differentiate your brand by developing a unique identity, voice, and customer experience. Clearly communicate your brand values and what sets you apart from the competition. By focusing on your unique qualities, you attract customers who align with your brand and are less swayed by competitive offerings.

Foster a Collaborative Culture: Nurture a culture of collaboration within your organization. Encourage teamwork, open communication, and the sharing of ideas. When your employees collaborate and support each other, they become more engaged, creative, and resilient in the face of competition.

Remember, competition is a natural part of the business landscape, and overcoming the fear associated with it is crucial for your success. Embrace collaboration, focus on delivering value, and continuously strive for improvement. When you adopt this mindset, you position yourself for growth, innovation, and long-term success in your industry.

Chapter 11

Creating an Ecosystem of Value

Now, let's explore the power of creating an ecosystem of value. Do you know that by building a network of partners and collaborators, you can enhance the value of your free offerings and drive growth and success for your business?

Collaboration is the key to creating an ecosystem of value. By joining forces with other businesses, you can leverage their expertise, resources, and networks to enhance the value you provide to your customers. Collaboration allows you to offer a more comprehensive solution, expand your reach, and tap into new markets.

Start by identifying potential partners who align with your mission, values, and target audience. Look for businesses that complement your offerings and can provide additional value to your customers. Consider their reputation, expertise, and the potential for a mutually beneficial relationship.

When approaching potential partners, focus on establishing agreements that create value for both parties. Seek win-win arrangements where each partner can leverage the strengths and resources of the other. This could include sharing customer referrals, co-developing products or services, or jointly marketing to a shared audience.

Collaborating with partners allows you to enhance the value of your free offerings. By integrating complementary products or services from your partners, you can provide a more comprehensive and compelling solution to your customers. This strengthens your competitive advantage and differentiates your offerings in the market.

Cross-promotion is a powerful strategy within an ecosystem of value. Partner with businesses that target similar customer segments but offer different products or services. By cross-promoting each other's offerings, you can expand your customer base and increase brand exposure. This collaborative marketing approach benefits all parties involved.

Collaborate with partners to co-create valuable content, resources, or educational materials. This could include webinars, ebooks, podcasts, or workshops. By pooling your expertise, you can deliver more comprehensive and impactful resources to your audience, positioning yourself as a go-to authority in your industry.

Explore opportunities to share distribution channels with your partners. This could involve featuring each other's offerings on your websites, co-hosting events, or participating in joint ventures. Sharing distribution channels enables you to tap into each other's networks and reach a wider audience, creating new opportunities for growth.

Implement customer referral programs in collaboration with your partners. Encourage your satisfied customers to refer their friends and colleagues to both your business and your partners. In return, offer incentives or rewards that benefit both the referring customer and the new customer. This collaborative approach expands your customer base and strengthens customer loyalty.

Join forces with partners to conduct research and development initiatives. By pooling resources and expertise, you can innovate, solve complex problems, and bring new products or services to market faster.

Collaborative R&D fosters creativity, drives innovation, and positions your business at the forefront of your industry.

Maintain open lines of communication with your partners to ensure that the collaboration remains fruitful. Regularly evaluate the outcomes and impact of your collaborative efforts and make adjustments as needed. This iterative approach allows you to refine your strategies and maximize the value created within your ecosystem.

Remember, creating an ecosystem of value is about leveraging the strengths and resources of your partners to enhance the value you provide to your customers. Collaboration amplifies your impact, expands your reach, and drives growth and success for all parties involved. Embrace the power of collaboration and start building your ecosystem of value today. Here are a few additional points to consider:

Foster a culture of trust and transparency within your collaborative partnerships. Clearly communicate expectations, goals, and responsibilities from the outset. Trust is the foundation of successful collaborations, and transparency helps maintain alignment and mutual understanding.

Building strong relationships with your partners is essential for long-term success. Regularly engage with them, provide support, and seek opportunities for collaboration. Nurturing these relationships fosters loyalty and strengthens the foundation of your ecosystem of value.

Be open to adapting and adjusting your collaboration strategies as the needs of your partners and the market change. Flexibility allows you to seize new opportunities, respond to challenges, and pivot when necessary. Embrace a mindset of continuous learning and improvement to stay agile within your ecosystem.

Develop key performance indicators (KPIs) to measure the impact of your collaborative efforts. Track metrics such as customer acquisition, revenue growth, customer satisfaction, and brand visibility. Regularly assess the results to understand the effectiveness of your collaborations and identify areas for improvement.

Celebrate the successes and milestones achieved within your ecosystem of value. Recognize the contributions of your partners and acknowledge the collective accomplishments. By celebrating together, you foster a positive and supportive environment that encourages ongoing collaboration and mutual growth.

Continuously seek new partners and collaborators to expand your ecosystem of value. Keep an eye on emerging businesses, industry trends, and market opportunities. Actively participate in industry events, conferences, and networking activities to connect with potential partners who can contribute to your ecosystem.

Infuse a culture of collaboration into your organization. Encourage employees to seek and embrace collaborative opportunities both internally and externally. Provide the necessary resources, tools, and incentives to support and reward collaborative efforts. A collaborative culture creates a fertile ground for innovation and growth.

Share your experiences, challenges, and learnings with other businesses and entrepreneurs. Contribute to the collective knowledge by participating in industry forums, writing articles, or speaking at conferences. By sharing your insights, you contribute to the growth of the broader business community and inspire others to embrace collaboration.

Seek partners and collaborators from diverse

backgrounds, perspectives, and experiences. Embracing diversity and inclusion within your ecosystem of value fosters innovation, creativity, and a broader understanding of customer needs. Embrace different viewpoints and leverage the power of collective wisdom.

A successful ecosystem of value is not static but evolves and adapts over time. Continuously assess the market landscape, customer needs, and emerging trends. Stay agile and be willing to iterate your collaborations, adding new partners, refining strategies, and exploring new opportunities. Embrace a growth mindset and be open to continuous improvement.

Remember, building an ecosystem of value through collaboration is a powerful strategy to drive growth and success. When you leverage the strengths and resources of your partners, you can enhance the value you offer to your customers and create a sustainable competitive advantage. Embrace the spirit of collaboration, nurture your relationships, and strive for collective success within your ecosystem of value.

Chapter 12
The Power of Free
Marketing

In today's digital age, word-of-mouth marketing has become more influential than ever before. When you harness the power of free offerings, you can create viral campaigns and generate buzz around your business. Free marketing can be harnessed via:

The Influence of Word-of-Mouth: Word-of-mouth marketing is one of the most powerful forms of advertising. When people hear positive recommendations from their friends, family, or trusted sources, they are more likely to take action. Free offerings provide an excellent opportunity to create positive word-of-mouth and generate organic buzz around your business.

Creating Remarkable Experiences: To harness the power of free marketing, focus on creating remarkable experiences for your customers. Whether it's a free product, service, or valuable content, make it stand out from the competition. Exceed expectations, deliver exceptional quality, and provide a memorable experience that people can't help but talk about.

The Viral Potential: Free offerings have the potential to go viral, spreading rapidly through social media platforms and online communities. Design your free campaigns with shareability in mind. Make it easy for people to share your offerings with their networks, and encourage them to do so by offering incentives or rewards.

Leveraging User-Generated Content: Encourage users

to create and share content related to your free offerings. User-generated content adds authenticity and social proof to your marketing efforts. People trust recommendations from their peers, so when they see others sharing their positive experiences with your free offerings, they are more likely to take notice and engage with your business.

Social Media Amplification: Social media platforms are a powerful tool for free marketing. Leverage social media to amplify the reach of your free offerings. Create engaging and shareable content, host contests or giveaways, and actively engage with your audience. By fostering a community around your free offerings, you create a platform for organic sharing and engagement.

Influencer Collaborations: Collaborating with influencers can significantly amplify your free marketing efforts. Identify influencers in your industry who align with your brand and target audience. Engage them in your free campaigns and encourage them to share their experiences with their followers. Influencers have a loyal following and their endorsements can create a massive impact on your brand's visibility and reputation.

Referral Programs: Implement referral programs as part of your free marketing strategy. Encourage your existing customers to refer their friends, family, or colleagues to avail themselves of your free offerings. Incentivize referrals with rewards or exclusive benefits. Referral programs leverage the power of personal recommendations and encourage organic growth.

Leveraging Reviews and Testimonials: Positive reviews and testimonials are invaluable for free marketing. Encourage your customers to leave reviews or share testimonials about their experience with your free offerings. Display these reviews prominently on your website, social media profiles, and other marketing channels. Testimonials provide social proof and build trust among potential customers.

Collaborative Campaigns: Collaborate with complementary businesses or organizations to create joint marketing campaigns centered around free offerings. Pool your resources, creativity, and networks to create a buzz that benefits all parties involved. Collaborative campaigns have the potential to reach a wider audience and generate increased visibility and engagement.

Storytelling: Use storytelling techniques to create compelling narratives around your free offerings. Craft a captivating story that resonates with your target audience and highlights the value they can derive from your offerings. Storytelling evokes emotions, captures attention, and makes your brand more memorable, increasing the chances of people sharing your story with others.

Embrace Social Sharing: Make it easy for people to share your free offerings on social media platforms. Incorporate social sharing buttons or prompts into your website, content, and emails. Encourage users to share their experiences and provide social media templates or hashtags that align with your campaign. Amplify the reach of your free offerings through the power of social sharing.

Utilize Influencer Marketing: Collaborate with influencers who have a strong presence in your industry or target market. Influencers can help create awareness and generate buzz around your free offerings by sharing their experiences and endorsing your brand. Choose influencers whose values align with yours and who have an engaged and relevant audience.

Engage with Your Audience: Actively engage with your audience and foster meaningful conversations. Respond to comments, messages, and reviews related to your free offerings. Show genuine interest in their experiences and address any concerns or questions promptly. Building a strong connection with your audience cultivates trust, loyalty, and positive word-of-mouth.

Create Share-Worthy Content: Develop content that is highly shareable and provides value to your audience. This can include informative articles, how-to guides, entertaining videos, or visually appealing infographics. Craft content that is not only valuable but also encourages people to share it with their networks, expanding the reach of your free offerings.

Encourage User-Generated Content: Inspire your audience to create and share content related to your free offerings. Run contests or challenges that encourage users to share their experiences, stories, or creative interpretations. This user-generated content serves as authentic testimonials and provides social proof that can inspire others to engage with your business.

Leverage Online Communities: Identify relevant online communities, forums, or groups where your target audience congregates. Become an active participant and provide value by sharing insights, answering questions, and offering assistance. Position yourself as an expert and subtly promote your free offerings when relevant. Engaging in these communities helps build trust and credibility, leading to increased word-of-mouth recommendations.

Collaboration with Nonprofits or Causes: Partner with nonprofits or support meaningful causes aligned with your brand values. Offer your free products or services to support their initiatives or donate a portion of your revenue. This collaboration not only generates positive publicity but also taps into the networks and communities associated with the nonprofit, expanding the reach of your free offerings.

Leverage Customer Advocacy: Cultivate a community of loyal customers who act as advocates for your brand. Offer exclusive benefits or rewards to customers who actively promote your free offerings. Encourage them to share their positive experiences, provide testimonials, or refer others. Customer advocates can become influential brand ambassadors and drive significant word-of-mouth marketing.

Continuous Optimization: Regularly evaluate the effectiveness of your free marketing strategies and optimize them based on the data and feedback you receive. Analyze metrics such as referral traffic, social media engagement, conversion rates, and customer feedback. Use these insights to refine your approach, identify areas for improvement, and amplify the impact of your free offerings.

Remember, the power of free marketing lies in its ability to create a buzz, generate excitement, and ignite conversations about your business. When you implement these strategies and foster an environment where people willingly share their positive experiences, you can tap into the immense potential of word-of-mouth marketing.

The key is to create remarkable experiences, leverage social sharing, collaborate with influencers and complementary businesses, and continuously engage with your audience.

As you implement these strategies, keep in mind the importance of tracking and measuring your results. Monitor the impact of your free marketing efforts through analytics and feedback from customers. This data will provide valuable insights into what is working and what can be improved, allowing you to iterate and optimize your approach over time.

Chapter 13

Free as a Business Model

I know you run a real estate business, or any kind of business and you are wondering how you can adopt all that you have learnt in this book. Now, we will look at businesses that have adopted a free business model. These companies have defied conventional wisdom by giving away their products or services for free, and yet, they have achieved remarkable success.

One popular approach to the free business model is the "freemium" model, where a basic version of the product or service is offered for free, while premium features or advanced functionalities come at a cost. Companies like Spotify and Dropbox have successfully utilized this model, enticing users with free access and then converting them into paying customers by offering additional value.

Some companies offer free products or services and generate revenue through advertising. Google, with its suite of free tools like Search, Maps, and Gmail, monetizes through targeted advertising. These companies understand that by providing valuable free offerings, they attract a large user base, which in turn becomes an attractive platform for advertisers.

Companies like Facebook and Instagram provide their platforms for free, collecting vast amounts of user data in the process. They then monetize this data by offering targeted advertising opportunities to businesses. This data-driven approach highlights the value of free offerings in capturing user information and leveraging it for monetization.

Some businesses employ a free business model to create network effects, where the more users join the platform, the more valuable it becomes for all users. Social media platforms like Facebook and LinkedIn thrive on this principle, offering free access to their platforms to attract and retain a massive user base, which in turn drives engagement and creates value for users and advertisers alike.

The open-source model fosters collaboration and innovation by allowing developers and users to freely access and modify software code. Companies like WordPress and Mozilla Firefox have leveraged open-source principles to create powerful, widely adopted products while nurturing communities of contributors. The free nature of open-source software encourages participation, resulting in continuous improvement and widespread adoption.

Platforms like YouTube and Medium provide free

access to user-generated content while monetizing through advertising or subscription models. By offering a platform for content creators to reach a broad audience, these companies create a mutually beneficial ecosystem where users can access valuable content for free, and creators can earn revenue through various monetization channels.

Companies often give away certain products or services for free to drive sales or adoption of other related offerings. For instance, video game developers may offer free demos or limited versions to attract players and encourage them to purchase the full game. This strategy allows businesses to showcase the value of their offerings and convert free users into paying customers.

Free offerings can serve as powerful tools for brand building and customer acquisition. Companies like HubSpot and Canva offer free versions of their software tools, allowing users to experience the value and benefits firsthand. As users become familiar with the product and its capabilities, they are more likely to upgrade to paid plans or recommend the product to others.

Some businesses adopt a free business model to focus on long-term value and customer lifetime revenue. By providing free products or services, they build trust, loyalty, and a strong customer base. These companies understand that while the initial transaction may be free, the lifetime value of a customer extends far beyond that, with potential upsells, cross-sells, and repeat purchases.

Free business models often challenge established industries and disrupt traditional business models. Companies like Skype and WhatsApp disrupted the telecommunications industry by offering free or low-cost communication services, revolutionizing the way people connect and communicate. These disruptive innovations demonstrate the power of thinking differently and leveraging the concept of free to challenge existing norms and create new market opportunities.

Businesses that adopt a free business model understand the importance of network effects in driving growth and value creation. They focus on attracting a critical mass of users by offering free access to their platforms, products, or services. As the user base grows, the value of the offering increases, creating a positive feedback loop that attracts even more users and enhances the overall experience for everyone involved.

Companies that embrace the free business model often seek strategic partnerships to enhance their offerings and expand their reach. By collaborating with complementary businesses, they can create synergies and unlock new growth opportunities. These partnerships may involve cross-promotion, co-creation of content or products, or joint marketing efforts, all aimed at leveraging the power of free to attract and engage a broader audience.

Free offerings provide an opportunity to collect valuable customer data and gain insights into user behavior and preferences. Companies that adopt the free business model understand the importance of data in driving business decisions and improving their offerings. By analyzing user data, they can refine their strategies, personalize experiences, and create targeted marketing campaigns that resonate with their audience.

Embracing the free business model requires a mindset of innovation and adaptability. Successful companies continuously innovate their offerings, explore new revenue streams, and adapt to changing market dynamics. They understand that the free business model is not static but requires ongoing evolution to stay competitive and relevant in a rapidly changing business landscape.

Create a Community: Free offerings have the power to create vibrant communities of users who share common interests, goals, or values. Companies that cultivate a sense of community around their free offerings foster engagement, collaboration, and loyalty among their users. This community becomes a valuable asset, contributing to the growth and success of the business through advocacy, user-generated content, and word-of-mouth referrals.

As you explore the stories and lessons of successful companies that have adopted the free business model, remember that each business has its unique journey and strategies. What works for one may not work for another. However, by understanding the principles and insights derived from these examples, you can apply them to your own business context and uncover new opportunities for growth and success.

The free business model challenges traditional notions of commerce and demonstrates that value can be created and monetized in innovative ways. As you embark on your entrepreneurial journey, consider how the concept of free can be leveraged strategically to differentiate your business, attract a loyal customer base, and ultimately drive sustainable revenue and success.

The Ethics of Free

In today's business landscape, the concept of giving away products and services for free has gained significant traction. While it presents numerous opportunities for businesses, it also raises important ethical considerations. Let us look at some of these considerations so we can better navigate the complexities of offering free goods and services while upholding integrity and social responsibility.

Honesty and Transparency:

When implementing a free business model, it is crucial to maintain honesty and transparency with customers. Clearly communicate the terms and conditions of the free offer, including any limitations, fees, or obligations that may arise later. Avoid deceptive practices or hidden costs that could erode trust and damage your reputation.

Balancing Value and Sustainability:

Offering products or services for free requires striking a balance between providing value to customers and ensuring the long-term sustainability of your business. Evaluate the costs and benefits of your free offerings to ensure they align with your overall business objectives. Consider how free offerings can be financially viable without compromising the quality or value provided to customers.

Fairness and Equality:

Consider the potential impact of free offerings on fairness and equality. Ensure that your free offerings do not discriminate against certain groups or perpetuate societal inequalities. Strive for inclusivity and equal access to your free offerings, considering the diverse needs and circumstances of your target audience.

Social and Environmental Responsibility:

While focusing on the benefits of offering free products and services, it is essential to consider the broader social and environmental implications. Evaluate how your business practices align with sustainable development goals and ethical standards. Minimize any negative impact on the environment, respect human rights, and contribute positively to the communities you serve.

Value Exchange:

Even in free offerings, there should be a value exchange between your business and customers. While customers may not pay with money, they provide valuable data, feedback, or other forms of engagement. Respect the value of their contributions and use it responsibly to improve your offerings and deliver greater value to your customers.

Long-Term Relationships:

Free offerings can be an opportunity to build long-term relationships with customers. Focus on fostering trust, engagement, and loyalty. Continuously provide value and ensure that your free offerings are not just a short-term marketing ploy, but rather a genuine commitment to customer satisfaction and success.

Social Impact:

Consider the potential positive social impact of your free offerings. Look beyond immediate business goals and explore how your products or services can address social challenges, contribute to community development, or support charitable causes. Aligning your free offerings with a higher purpose can enhance your reputation and create a positive societal impact.

Collaboration and Partnerships:

Engage in collaborative efforts with other organizations or nonprofits to amplify the impact of your free offerings. Partnering with like-minded entities can extend your reach, create synergies, and drive collective social or environmental change.

Chapter 14

Embracing Abundance: A Personal Transformation

Let us embark on a transformative journey to shift your personal beliefs and mindset towards abundance and generosity. The truth is that by overcoming scarcity thinking and embracing the potential for unlimited growth, you can unlock new opportunities, foster prosperity, and experience personal fulfillment. To achieve this, we must pay attention to these:

Recognizing Scarcity Thinking:

The first step towards embracing abundance is to recognize any patterns of scarcity thinking that may be holding you back. Scarcity thinking is rooted in the belief that resources, opportunities, and success are limited, leading to a mindset of fear, competition, and hoarding. Become aware of any scarcity-based thoughts or beliefs that may be limiting your potential.

Shifting to an Abundance Mindset:

Embracing an abundance mindset involves reframing your beliefs and perceptions about the world. Understand that there is an abundance of resources, opportunities, and possibilities available to you. Instead of viewing success as a zero-sum game, adopt the belief that there is enough for everyone to thrive and succeed.

Gratitude and Appreciation:

Cultivating gratitude and appreciation is a powerful tool for embracing abundance. Take time each day to reflect on the blessings, opportunities, and abundance that already exists in your life. Focus on the positive aspects and express gratitude for the people, experiences, and resources that contribute to your well-being and growth.

Letting Go of Scarcity Mentality:

To fully embrace abundance, it is essential to let go of the scarcity mentality that may be holding you back. Release fears, doubts, and limiting beliefs that stem from scarcity thinking. Replace them with empowering beliefs that align with abundance, such as "There are endless possibilities available to me" or "I am deserving of success and abundance."

Abundance as a State of Being:

Shift your perception of abundance from an external condition to an internal state of being. Recognize that abundance is not solely determined by external factors, such as wealth or possessions, but also by your mindset, attitude, and the richness of your relationships and experiences. Embrace the idea that abundance starts within you.

Cultivating Generosity:

One of the most powerful ways to embrace abundance is through generosity. Practice acts of kindness, giving, and sharing without expecting anything in return. By sharing your time, resources, and talents with others, you create a positive cycle of abundance that flows back to you in unexpected ways.

Abundance and Unlimited Growth:

Embrace the belief that your potential for growth and success is unlimited. Understand that abundance is not finite but can expand exponentially as you tap into your creativity, develop new skills, and seize opportunities. Embrace a growth mindset that allows you to continuously learn, adapt, and evolve.

Collaboration and Abundance:

Recognize that collaboration and cooperation are integral to abundance. Instead of viewing others as competitors, seek opportunities for collaboration and partnership. By leveraging collective strengths and resources, you can create synergistic outcomes that benefit everyone involved.

Celebrating Abundance in Others:

Shift from envy or comparison to celebrating the abundance in others. Recognize that someone else's success does not diminish your own. Celebrate the achievements and prosperity of others, as their abundance serves as a reminder of what is possible for you as well.

Abundance as a Ripple Effect:

Understand that embracing abundance not only

transforms your own life but also has a ripple effect on others and the world around you. Your mindset and actions can inspire and uplift others, creating a positive impact that extends beyond yourself.

As you cultivate an abundance mindset, you become a magnet for positive experiences and opportunities that align with your desires and aspirations. Embracing abundance is a lifelong journey that requires consistent practice and self-reflection.

Be patient with yourself as you navigate the transformation process, and celebrate every step forward, no matter how small. As you continue to embrace abundance and let go of scarcity thinking, you will unleash your true potential, attract abundant opportunities, and create a life of fulfillment and prosperity.

Chapter 15

Shifting Personal Beliefs
and Mindset Towards
Abundance and Generosity
as a Business Person

As a business person, it is crucial to adopt an abundance mindset that recognizes the limitless opportunities and resources available. Shift your beliefs from scarcity to abundance. Rather than viewing competitors as threats, reframe your perspective to see them as collaborators and catalysts for growth.

Embrace the idea that there is room for everyone to succeed and that healthy competition can inspire innovation and push you to reach new heights. Cultivate a mindset that seeks to collaborate, learn from others, and build mutually beneficial relationships.

Focusing on Value Creation. Shift your focus from solely pursuing profits to creating value for your customers, employees, and stakeholders. Embrace the belief that by genuinely serving and providing value to others, you will attract more opportunities and foster long-term success. Seek to understand the needs and desires of your target market and consistently innovate to meet those needs.

Cultivating a Spirit of Generosity. Incorporate generosity into your business practices by giving freely and selflessly. This can take various forms, such as providing free resources, offering pro bono services, or supporting charitable causes. Embrace the belief that acts of generosity not only benefit others but also create a positive impact on your business by building trust, loyalty, and goodwill.

Abundant Thinking in Decision-Making. When making business decisions, approach them with an abundant mindset rather than a scarcity mindset. Avoid making decisions rooted in fear or a sense of lack. Instead, focus on the possibilities, opportunities, and potential outcomes that align with your vision of abundance. Trust in your abilities and have faith that the resources needed to support your decisions will manifest.

Embracing Failure and Learning. Shift your perspective on failure from a setback to a valuable learning experience. Embrace the belief that failure is a stepping stone towards growth and success. Learn from your mistakes, iterate, and adapt your strategies to create better outcomes. Embracing a growth mindset allows you to approach challenges with resilience, perseverance, and a focus on continuous improvement.

Building Collaborative Networks. Recognize the power of collaboration and build networks of like-minded individuals, entrepreneurs, and professionals. Surround yourself with individuals who share an abundance mindset and are willing to support and uplift each other. Collaborative networks can provide valuable insights, opportunities for partnership, and a supportive community that fosters growth and success.

Practicing Gratitude and Celebration. Cultivate a practice of gratitude and celebrate your achievements along the way. Express gratitude for the opportunities, successes, and partnerships that come your way. Celebrate milestones and accomplishments, no matter how small, as they contribute to the overall abundance and growth of your business. Gratitude and celebration amplify positive energy and attract more abundance into your life.

When you consciously shift your personal beliefs and

mindset towards abundance and generosity as a business person, you open yourself up to a world of possibilities and create a positive impact on your business and those around you. Embrace an abundance mindset, cultivate a spirit of generosity, and approach challenges and opportunities with resilience and gratitude.

Chapter 16

The Future of Free

L et us dive into the future of free and examine how the business landscape is evolving in relation to giving away everything for free. As technology advances, consumer behaviors shift, and new market trends emerge, it is essential to stay ahead of the curve and adapt to the changing dynamics. Let's peep into the future of free and uncover predictions and trends that will shape the business landscape:

Hyper-Personalization:

In the future, free offerings will become more personalized and tailored to individual needs and preferences. Advanced technologies such as artificial intelligence and machine learning will enable businesses to gather and analyze vast amounts of data, allowing them to deliver highly targeted and relevant free products, services, and content. Personalization will enhance the user experience, build stronger connections, and drive customer loyalty.

Freemium Models:

Freemium models, which offer basic services for free while charging for premium features, will continue to gain popularity. This approach allows businesses to attract a wide user base with free offerings while monetizing through value-added features or exclusive content. As consumers become accustomed to accessing free services, the freemium model provides an opportunity to upsell and generate revenue from a loyal customer base.

Data as Currency:

Data has become a valuable currency in the digital age.

As businesses give away free products or services, they collect valuable user data, which can be leveraged for targeted marketing, product development, and decision-making. In the future, businesses will find innovative ways to extract insights from user data and create personalized experiences that drive engagement and conversion.

Collaborative Partnerships:

Collaboration and strategic partnerships will play a significant role in the future of free. Businesses will form alliances to pool resources, expand their reach, and offer more comprehensive free offerings. Collaborative partnerships can lead to shared databases, cross-promotion, and joint marketing efforts, ultimately benefiting both the businesses involved and the end-users.

Blockchain and Tokenization:

Blockchain technology and tokenization have the potential to revolutionize the future of free. By leveraging blockchain, businesses can create decentralized platforms where users are rewarded with tokens for their engagement, feedback, and participation. These tokens can be exchanged for additional benefits, access to premium features, or even tradable assets, providing a new level of value and incentive for users.

User-Generated Content and Crowdsourcing:

The future of free will see an increased emphasis on user-generated content and crowdsourcing. Businesses will harness the power of their user communities to create and curate valuable content, feedback, and ideas. User-generated content adds authenticity, diversity, and engagement to free offerings, building a sense of ownership and fostering a strong community.

Sustainability and Social Impact:

As consumers become more conscious of sustainability and social impact, the future of free will see businesses aligning their offerings with these values. Companies will incorporate environmental and social responsibility into their free offerings, demonstrating their commitment to making a positive difference in the world. Free products and services will not only serve a functional purpose but also contribute to a larger cause, resonating with consumers who prioritize sustainability and social impact.

Augmented Reality and Virtual Reality:

Emerging technologies such as augmented reality (AR) and virtual reality (VR) will reshape the future of free by offering immersive and interactive experiences. Businesses will provide free AR and VR experiences to engage users, showcase products, and create memorable interactions. This technology will revolutionize the way users consume content, try out products virtually, and make informed purchasing decisions.

The future of free is an exciting and dynamic landscape; one that is driven by evolving consumer expectations, technological advancements, and changing market trends. As a business person, you need to look forward to this phase.

Stay abreast of these trends and adapt your strategies accordingly. Doing so, you will position yourself as a forward-thinking and customer-centric business person. Stay open to innovation, experiment with new strategies, and be willing to adapt and evolve with the changing times.

The future holds immense potential for those who are

willing to embrace the transformative power of giving away everything for free while staying attuned to the needs and desires of their customers.